GO/ LS	01/15			

Goring Library
Station Road
Goring
Oxon RG8 9HA
Tel: 01491 873028

e-
in
er
lp
es

To renew this book, phone 0845 1202811 or visit
our website at www.libcat.oxfordshire.gov.uk
You will need your library PIN number
(available from your library)

Caversham Court Gardens
A Heritage Guide

by Friends of Caversham Court Gardens

TWO RIVERS PRESS

First published in the UK in 2012 by Two Rivers Press Ltd.
7 Denmark Road, Reading RG1 5PA
www.tworiverspress.com

ISBN 978-1-901677-86-7

1 2 3 4 5 6 7 8 9

Two Rivers Press is represented in the UK by Inpress Ltd and distributed
by Central Books.

Cover and text design by Nadja Guggi and typeset in Parisine and Janson.

Back cover: The roundels are found on various gates and are representative
of past families and features of the Gardens. Top to bottom: Simonds,
kitchen garden, Loveday, secret garden, griffins, St Peter's Church.

Printed and bound in Great Britain by Ashford Colour Press, Gosport.

ACKNOWLEDGEMENTS

Vickie Abel, Gillian Clark, Les Gibson and Anne White would like to thank Two Rivers Press, particularly Sally Mortimore, Nadja Guggi, Barbara Morris and Adam Sowan, without whom there would have been no book; the staff of all the record offices but particularly those of Caversham and Reading Central Library, the Local Studies Library, the University of Reading Museum of English Rural Life and the Berkshire Records Office, for their generous help and advice throughout this project; Dennis Alder for information about his grandfather Thomas Wareham, gardener to Lady Mosley, and the gift to the Friends of a photograph album of the gardens presented by her to Thomas on his retirement; Gill Learner for her poem and Mary Phelan for her drawing of the kiosk; and the many friends and supporters who have provided photographs, shared their knowledge and given help where it was needed. Overseas, Beverly Sutley of the Palmer Museum of Art was extremely helpful in enabling some of the original Loveday portraits to be used.

Particular mention is made of Brian Adsolom, David Arathoon, David Cliffe, Mike Cooper, Alison Hewitt, Carolyn Jenkins, Anne Keenan, Helen Lambert, Claire McWilliam, Francis Markham, John Markham, Raymond Simonds and Judith Still whose contributions made all the difference. Les Gibson provided many of the modern photographs (including those used for the cover) and also managed the project for the Friends.

The contributions of the following to the preparation of this heritage guide are acknowledged with thanks: the Caversham Court Gazebo Trust, Heritage Lottery Fund, Friends of Caversham Court Gardens, Caversham 100 Years On.

Foreword

Around a small dwelling, once used by priests, on the banks of the River Thames in Caversham, a grand old house and gardens renowned for their beauty grew up. The splendid former rectory of St Peter's Church has long been demolished, but its tranquil grounds are open to the public, and were recently restored by Reading Borough Council, with £1.2 million assistance from the Heritage Lottery Fund.

Caversham Court has a 950-year history. While changes to the site happened slowly, some were very significant. This book tells the story of the people who lived here, and their nurturing, neglect or transformation of this site. It also chronicles the recent restoration of the Gardens.

Planning the restoration was complex. The layers of history, from the eleventh to the twenty-first centuries, needed to be discovered, exposed, restored and interpreted. The vision was to bind together these old and private layers to create a public garden with a timeless sense of peace.

Other factors heightened the complexity in getting the design right. All gardens need to delight those who wander in them, but these Gardens are not only seen from within; they are looked 'down on' and 'across at', and the composition must also give pleasure from above and from across the river. There is nothing here by chance, and it is the hope of the authors of this book that your enjoyment will be so much the greater for what you find out.

This book is the work of the Friends of Caversham Court Gardens. They have researched it and written it, unearthing fascinating bits of information about the people associated with the former rectory and its grounds. They join me in thanking Anne Keenan for her careful collection of information during the restoration project, which has been invaluable in writing this book. And I thank them, for the interest they take, the time they invest, and the contribution that they make.

Some projects really are labours of love. The restoration of Caversham Court Gardens was one of these. The enjoyment of these Gardens by an ever increasing number of people will be love's labours secured. This book is offered as a contribution to that enjoyment.

Dr Carolyn Jenkins
Landscape architect
Parks Development Manager, Reading Borough Council

Introduction

Caversham Court Gardens lie on the north bank of the River Thames, near Caversham Bridge. Originally belonging to a private house on the river bank, the Gardens have a sense of intimacy and seclusion that explains why some describe them as 'Caversham's best kept secret'. But they have not always been so inconspicuous. Many interesting people and important families have lived there and have left behind them tantalising clues to their past. These have been unearthed and drawn upon in the design of the newly-restored public space to give it a unique and very personal character. The house, or rather, its residents, made the Gardens what they are today and this guide will introduce you to some of them, demonstrating how their influence on the development of the Gardens extends to the present day.

The earliest-known house on the site was built, like Reading Abbey, in the twelfth century. It was replaced by a Tudor house and this, in its turn, was substantially remodelled in Victorian times. The site was bought by Reading Borough Council in the 1930s and the last house demolished in 1933 and its garden opened to the public. In 2004 the Council, with the support of Heritage Lottery funding, began a complete reconstruction of the site and added back footprints of both the houses – outlines of the rooms in brick and stone which can be walked around and over. The Gardens re-opened after a year's closure in 2009.

All the owners and occupants of the property from 1586 to 1933 are known and two of them, the Dean and Chapter of Christ Church, Oxford, and Reading Borough Council, have in their care documents about its management that cover that entire period. Sale catalogues for the house in 1799, 1909, 1911 and 1933 provide useful marker points as do maps and the 1910 Inland Revenue property survey. There are also rich sources of stories about the people who lived there. Three of the principal occupiers of the houses, William Alexander (or Milward), John Loveday and the Simonds family (Reading bankers and brewers), have left written evidence about their lives there, not just the births, marriages and deaths in the parish registers and the decadal censuses, but wills, probate inventories and marriage settlements, insurance policies, legal papers from personal and business court cases, a published diary and family letters, press reports of events on the site, business records and photographs. Some of the head gardeners who worked there have been traced and their contributions also included in the story.

Different titles were given to the house and garden over time and across documents and sources, sometimes applied to the entire property, sometimes to its purpose or appearance, sometimes as an address. 'Rectory', 'Old Rectory' (or just 'old rectory') were commonly used; 'Parsonage' and 'the Striped House' less so. All except the last were linked to the right of the owner or the lay tenant to appoint the priest at St Peter's and to the right to the tithes from the parish. The guide reflects this variety but recognises that in the twentieth century the return to 'Old Rectory' (in the sense of 'former rectory') marked a break with the church and the beginning of the lay ownership which continues with 'Caversham Court'.

In order to give an overview of the chronology of the guide, the timeline on the opposite page shows how local occurrences correspond with national and international events. In the Gardens themselves, there is a timeline embedded in the causeway to the gazebo allowing visitors to fit people and events into a broader perspective.

As well as the historical dimension, this guide needs to provide a spatial perspective on the Gardens as they were, and are today. The houses on the site overlooked terraced lawns and trees along the river bank. A long walk still extends along the back of the lawn and leads, via a causeway, to the gazebo (or summer house) and to the site of the wet boathouse, passing steps whose posts bear some medieval corbels. Behind the long walk, the former kitchen garden is protected by an established yew hedge and on its far side by a long brick wall, built in concave sections. The wall has the double benefit of providing warmth for ripening fruit and preventing the churchyard from falling into the vegetable garden! It extends to a wall with heating ducts along the back of the vegetable garden that in Victorian days supported a row of greenhouses. An arch in the main garden wall carries a date of 1551 and an

A broad line runs the length of the causeway to the gazebo and is divided into metre lengths, each representing 100 years. On one side are national or international events and on the other are those connected with the house. Marking the causeway like this gives children a perspective on the length of time between events and it is also a very popular place for bridal photos to be taken after the wedding party leaves St Peter's. The limestone seats and the box plants make an attractive colour contrast.

The timeline looking towards the gazebo.

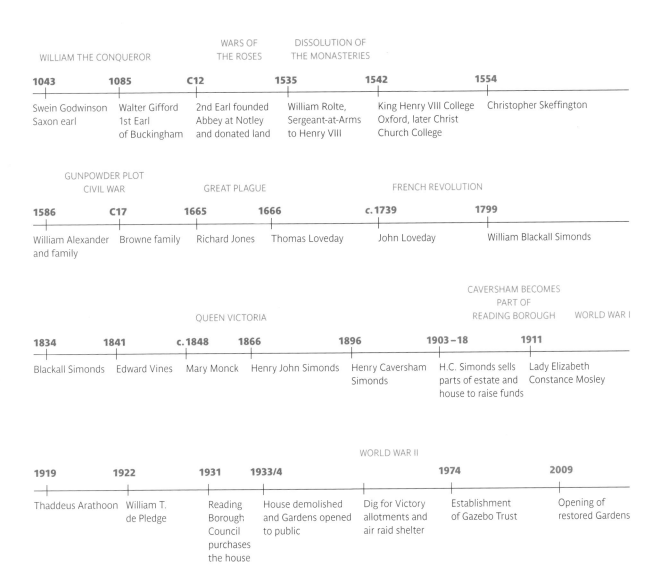

| | WARS OF | DISSOLUTION OF | | |
| WILLIAM THE CONQUEROR | THE ROSES | THE MONASTERIES | | |

1043	1085	C12	1535	1542	1554
Swein Godwinson Saxon earl	Walter Gifford 1st Earl of Buckingham	2nd Earl founded Abbey at Notley and donated land	William Rolte, Sergeant-at-Arms to Henry VIII	King Henry VIII College Oxford, later Christ Church College	Christopher Skeffington

| GUNPOWDER PLOT | | | | | |
| CIVIL WAR | | GREAT PLAGUE | | FRENCH REVOLUTION | |

1586	C17	1665	1666	c.1739	1799
William Alexander and family	Browne family	Richard Jones	Thomas Loveday	John Loveday	William Blackall Simonds

| | | | | CAVERSHAM BECOMES PART OF | |
| | | QUEEN VICTORIA | | READING BOROUGH | WORLD WAR I |

1834	1841	c.1848	1866	1896	1903–18	1911
Blackall Simonds	Edward Vines	Mary Monck	Henry John Simonds	Henry Caversham Simonds	H.C. Simonds sells parts of estate and house to raise funds	Lady Elizabeth Constance Mosley

| | | | WORLD WAR II | | |

1919	1922	1931	1933/4	1974	2009
Thaddeus Arathoon	William T. de Pledge	Reading Borough Council purchases the house	House demolished and Gardens opened to public	Dig for Victory allotments and air raid shelter	Establishment of Gazebo Trust	Opening of restored Gardens

The timeline records the names of known residents of the
dwellings on the site from medieval times until the 1930s.

outbuilding behind the house, once a barn and later stables, has Tudor brickwork in it. A brewhouse and laundry used to stand alongside. The plan opposite shows many of these features and enables the visitor or reader to understand the layout of the garden and identify textual references. Historical stories have been intentionally intermingled with descriptions of the plants and hard landscaping in the Gardens to show how the one influenced the other, but garden features are separated typographically from the historical text to help readers differentiate between the two.

The property that is now Caversham Court has a heritage derived from its buildings, its gardens and the lives of the people who lived there. It responded to changes in style and fashion and to outside events. We hope that this guidebook will let the reader share that heritage and so add to the pleasure of visiting the Gardens.

1. Entrance gate
2. Mulberry Court and Stanton air raid shelter
3. Footprints showing the layouts of the Loveday and Simonds houses
4. Stable yard
5. Head Gardener's office
6. Gallery garden
7. Churchyard gate
8. Long walk and Grade II listed retaining wall
9. Vinery and pond
10. WC
11. Tea kiosk
12. Lawn
13. Griffin Steps
14. Riverside walk
15. Gazebo
16. Secret garden
17. Causeway
18. Kitchen garden (restricted access)
19. Curved bay and buttress wall
20. Western gardens (restricted access)
21. Heated wall
22. Lavender bank
23. Screen wall
24. Fruit trees
25. Site of wet boathouse

Based on plan, Reading Borough Council, 2009

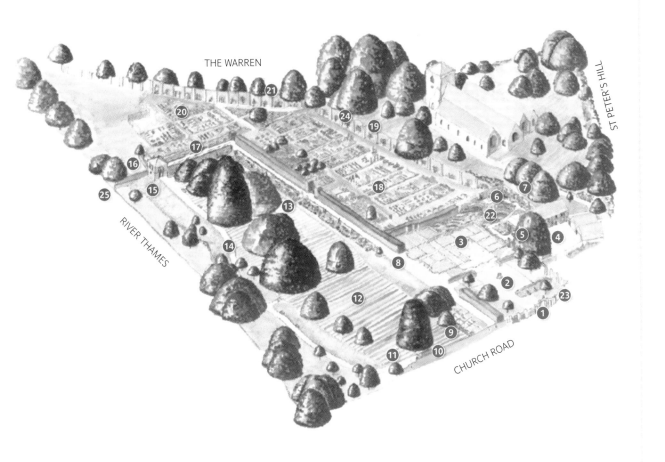

THE WARREN

ST PETER'S HILL

RIVER THAMES

CHURCH ROAD

The Rectory

In 1162 Walter Gifford, second Earl of Buckingham, founded an Augustinian religious house, Notley Abbey, at Long Crendon in Buckinghamshire. The money to run it came from a number of churches on his estate (land which had been given to his grandfather by William the Conqueror), of which St Peter's was one. The tithes of those churches, local taxes levied on personal and agricultural wealth in the parishes, were 'impropriated' to the use of the religious house. William, Earl Marshal, first Earl of Pembroke, later added a further gift to Notley Abbey of the garden and two acres of land which lay between the churchyard and the river. So the first house on this site was occupied not by its aristocratic owners, but by the priest at St Peter's church, and was the Rectory.

Little is known about the Rectory's first 350 years, but in 1535 Notley Abbey gave a tenancy to land at Caversham to William Rolte, Sergeant-at-Arms to King Henry VIII, with the duty to provide a priest for the church. Between 1536 and 1541 Henry dissolved all the religious houses, taking their property and income for his own use. The holdings of Notley Abbey, including Caversham Rectory, went in 1542 to his own foundation, King Henry VIII College in Oxford, formerly Cardinal Wolsey's College. When this was re-founded in 1546 as Christ Church, its Dean and Chapter became the new owners of the Rectory. William Rolte's lease was renegotiated with

them in 1543 and in 1554 the holder was another man with royal connections, Christopher Skeffington, Clerk to the Royal Kitchens.

Each ornamental gate in the garden has a logo on it to explain its position. The cross on this one at the top of the steps is a reminder of the former link between garden, house and church.

The Old Rectory or Striped House

Once the Caversham property was in lay hands it became known as the 'Old Rectory' or 'Old Parsonage'. The year MDLI (1551) is carved into a stone over a carriage gate in the outer flint wall and this may be the date when a new house was built on the site. Its builder and early tenants are unknown, but its wood and plaster construction and its black and white appearance gave it the local name of the Striped House.

The first person who can be directly connected with the house is another lay tenant, William Alexander, also known as William Milward. He sold inherited property in Hertfordshire to Anthony Brigham in 1579 and was in Caversham by 1586. By then he was married to Katherine Warde of Hurst; both were in their forties and they had had ten children. Alexander was a Roman Catholic and he was a money lender by profession, with an enthusiasm for taking to court those who defaulted on their contracts or who opposed him.

The documents about some of these disputes are now in The National Archives at Kew and are a rich source of information about the Alexander family and about the property. One of these cases shows that the Old Rectory was substantial enough to provide its tenant with an income from the impropriated tithes, gave him stabling for his horses and storage for his crops and made him self-sufficient in meat, fruit, vegetables, bread and beer. This is what happened: by 1586 Alexander had sublet some of the property to William Skidmore, who in

This gate stands close to the stable block and has a date on the inner side of the archway.

The date over the gate is MDLI (1551).

The Striped House from a drawing made by Barbara Seton
in 1792. It was three storeys high with a tiled roof and tall
chimneys and built round a courtyard. The church tower
to the right of the house marks its position in the garden
and shows the direction it faced (Markham, 1984).

turn transferred his interest in the lease to Thomas Brigham, and in 1588 the issue about which parts of the estate the tenancy included came to court. The parchment record of the case provides a list of what it comprised:

> the mansion or dwelling house itself, the lesser barn called the wheat barn, the stable, the brew house, the malt house; the tenement ... the dove or culver house, the barn adjoining the church yard, the orchard and gardens and all the glebelands [impropriated land providing tithes], the Mount, the [enclosed rabbit] warren, the barn adjoining the warren, the chancel, the churchyard, the hides [units of plough land between 60 and 180 acres],

the Great Mede with the tithes of the same hides and the glebes and tithes of all such ground (TNA, C43/8/163 and C2/ELIZ/B25/42).

In 1605 Robert Newport, also a Catholic, was staying at the Striped House and had been there for a couple of years. On 6 November, the day after the Gunpowder Plot to blow up Parliament had been exposed, Newport's name appeared in State Papers on a list of possible suspects to be investigated, because he and plotter Thomas Percy were connected with each other through their employment by the Earl of Northumberland.

A small section of the parchment on which the case between Alexander and Brigham was recorded. William Alexander's name can be read in lines 2 and 4, William Skidmore's in 5; the wheat barns, stables, orchards and gardens appear in 7 and 8, and the tithes and hides in line 9.

The lavender bank, St Peter's church behind it and the steps to the church.

The lavender bank today fills a sunny corner between the site of the priest's house and the steps to the church. It is planted for year-round interest with box, lavender 'Hidcote', blue-flowered hyssop, dwarf purple berberis, grey/green-leafed *Ballota pseudodictamnus* and several different types of santolina or cotton lavender, but it is at its best in July when the lines of colour give the appearance of an Impressionist painting.

On the other side of the steps to the churchyard is the 'winter walk', with early-flowering bergenia or elephant's ears, and, near the wall, azara, a shrub with insignificant yellow flowers which have a delicious aroma of chocolate. There is also scented daphne and mahonia, the coloured stems of cornus, a winter-flowering clematis, euphorbia and viburnum along the walk and a magnolia at the foot of the steps. Later in the year there are pink and white autumn cyclamen.

The cluster of yews at the west end of the long border, close to the causeway, are self-propagated daughters of an earlier tree, now themselves of a great age. There is a long connection between yew trees and holy places and the original tree that was in the centre may well have been there when the Earl of Pembroke gave the site to Notley Abbey. An underplanting of snowdrops provides a beautiful contrast to the dark green foliage in early spring.

The cluster of yew trees below the causeway and the copper beech tree.

Not only did Alexander have a brew house but excavations carried out during the restoration revealed there were also Tudor beer cellars, and later, wine cellars underneath the house. These have now been filled in according to best archaeological practice and are underneath the house footprint.

William Alexander died in 1611 and his wife Katherine in 1617. In her will she appointed her sons William and Thomas as executors, and made bequests to her servants Goodwives Michell, Tristrame, Piggott and Alloway and to her maids Isabel Wydmoor and Margarett Palmer. Her clothing was to be shared between her daughter Martha and granddaughters Sarah Manning and Coleberry Milward. She wished to be buried in the chancel of St Peter's church, with money to be distributed on the day of her funeral to the poor and to the bell-ringers (TNA. PROB 11/130).

William Alexander and Robert Newport's entries on the timeline on the causeway.

The date 1638 was carved into a newel post in the Striped House but its significance is long forgotten, even though the staircase and post survived until demolition of the house in 1933. The post is now on display in Reading Museum but, contrary to legend, does not have bullet holes in it from the Civil War (REDMG:1971.86).

Life events of the Alexanders continued to be recorded in St Peter's parish register and to appear in local documents well into the 1640s. One source says they held a lease for the house until 1647. If so, then they were there during the Civil War between the Royalists and the Parliamentarians (1642–1646) when Reading was besieged by both sides and King Charles I was finally held in 1647 at Caversham Park. They would have been able to hear the guns and cannons firing and to see the fighting on Caversham Bridge. They must have been aware of the armies attacking and withdrawing just outside their walls, the pillaging of food, wood and metal from local people, the billeting of soldiers and the spread of typhus from the military camps into the civilian population.

The Alexanders were succeeded at the Old Rectory by the Brownes, another Catholic and Royalist family. George Browne, son of Sir George Browne of Shefford, married Elizabeth Blount of Mapledurham and was knighted by Charles II at his coronation. At his death the tenancy passed to his son John, who took the name Sir John Browne of Caversham when he was created a baronet in 1665. Richard Jones of Welford Park, Newbury, was then the tenant for a short time while his own house was being repaired.

The Griffin Steps (Grade II listed status) looking from the lawns to the long walk.
Each post has a medieval corbel on its inner face.

The wisteria on the wall behind the western
flower border. The wall has Grade II listed status.

The Griffin Steps

The steps lead from the long walk between the house and the gazebo, through the red brick retaining wall, to the terraced lawn below. The wall was built in the seventeenth century and probably rebuilt in the next. Recent repairs to it are noticeable and show the high quality of the match between old and new bricks. Wall and walk together support the yew hedge that shelters the kitchen garden, and the south-facing wall on either side of the steps has a wisteria planted against it. The gate behind the steps is a modern introduction that carries the griffin logo and gives access from the long walk to the kitchen garden. The narrow border below the yew trees is planted with catmint.

The piers at the head of the steps are each topped with the head of a griffin, a heraldic beast symbolising strength and vigilance, with the head, wings and feet of an eagle and the body and back legs of a lion. Here the beast is simplified to an eagle's head with ears, as it often is when designed to be an architectural decoration or supporting structure. There is no evidence of where the heads came from or who brought them into the Gardens, but the example on the right when looking up the steps is a recent replacement and the other is a repaired original. The white covering is a protective layer which will stay in position while the new stonework hardens.

The Romanesque corbel on the western gate post.

The griffin on the western gate post before it was restored.

Each of the piers on which the griffins sit has a beast's head corbel built into it, the oldest structures in the garden. 'Corbel' is an architectural term for a projecting structure that holds something in position above, as, for example, a bracket supports a shelf. The example in the west gatepost is a 'Beast head corbel of oolitic limestone. Catlike with deep-set bulging eyes with lids above and below, undrilled pupils, pointed ears, bulging cheeks and a double upper lip with a notch in the centre. The nose is damaged but appears narrow.' The other is similar 'except that the stone is badly eroded and there is a large recent loss in the lip area at the bottom. The eyes are lidless and not so deeply set, and the nose is broader' (www.crsbi.ac.uk).

Thomas Loveday (*c.* 1619–1681)

Detail from *View of Caversham through the Gateway* (1791) by Charles Tomkins (Number Eight of Views of Reading Abbey, Reading Borough Libraries). This extract from Tomkins' print shows St Peter's church with the parsonage, by now known as the Old Rectory or the Striped House, in front of it. Taken from the inner gateway at Reading Abbey, the view shows how rural the landscape was between the Abbey and Caversham.

Thomas Loveday was the first of his family to live in Caversham and started a period of Caversham Court's history that was to last for about 130 years. Born around 1619, Thomas was from a family of mercers based in Atherstone, Warwickshire. He had been an officer in the army of King Charles I and styled himself 'captain' for the rest of his life. In 1646 he left his brother to run the family business and went to London to become an apprentice to a successful goldsmith, Richard Hill. He remained there until 1653 when he was admitted to the Freedom of the Goldsmiths' Company. His standing must have been significant among the goldsmiths as he later went on to achieve several other distinctions within the Company.

His first marriage probably took place to Mrs Hill, the widow of his goldsmith apprenticeship Master, and when he went seeking a house outside London in 1665 was likely to have been looking for a family home. This was the height of the Great Plague in the city, and Thomas was not alone among businessmen and professionals in seeking a healthier home in the country. He came to what was then known as the old parsonage at Caversham, ideally located by the river Thames, but within travelling distance of London where he still owned property.

Thomas took over the lease from a Richard Jones, although he did not take up residence until February 1666. The timber and stucco ('Striped') house was owned by Christ Church, Oxford, and by this time

The ruinous state of the gazebo. The causeway was crumbling and completely overgrown, and door and window openings were boarded up (Anne Keenan January 2007).

The Gazebo Trust was set up in 1974 by representatives of Reading Civic Society, the Berkshire Archaeological Society and Reading District Council to preserve and restore the Caversham Court gazebo, which was by then in a ruinous state. Their campaign to raise funds and raise awareness of the heritage that was being lost eventually led to the bid to restore the gardens as a whole. The Gazebo Trust was dissolved in 2010, its main aims achieved. Today, the gazebo still gives fine views over the river and the upper storey contains information boards giving some of the history of Caversham Court.

The lower entrance to the gazebo, on the western wall, facing into what is now the 'secret garden' and the allotments, has a raised flint surround and is much more decorative than the entrance facing the ornamental gardens. This type of ornamentation, called rustication, was a fashionable feature of much English stonework in the seventeenth and eighteenth centuries. The brick bands in the flint wall do not align with the brick courses of the west wall, however, which suggests the rusticated surround may have been added later. This entrance was clearly designed to be seen when returning from a promenade through the lower storey of the gazebo to the western end of the estate, leading out onto the Warren towards Mapledurham. There are records of this walk being widened by John Loveday in the mid-eighteenth century.

Above: Though the weather vane bears the date 1663, the gazebo is thought to have been built earlier in the century. The present weather vane is a replica, dedicated to one of the local campaigners who fought to save the gazebo, Molly Casey. The vane used as a model, now in St Peter's Church, was made of copper and partly gilded, though it was later covered in a black coating. The design incorporates fleurs de lys at the top and a finial of a Stuart thistle. It is not known for certain whether this one originally topped the gazebo.

Left: In line with modern conservation practice, the ground floor of the gazebo has been stabilised rather than restored, to show the original fabric of the building as it was found.

This painting of St Peter's from Caversham Bridge by the English landscape painter
Edmund Havell Senior (1785–1864) shows a gilded weather vane glinting on top of the gazebo
(REDMG:1998.180.53).

The original roof timbers have been re-used;
the under sides of the ceiling joists have
many small nail holes and linear marks from
a former lath and plaster ceiling.

During the restoration work on the causeway leading to the gazebo, an earlier dressed chalk, or clunch, wall was discovered in between the two brick and flint-faced walls which have been there since Tudor times. The original causeway may have been made by throwing earth against an old garden wall, perhaps when the site was terraced. When this wall could not stand the weight of the causeway, a new clunch and brick wall may have been built to reinforce the original one.

The two walls of the causeway were pinned together with steel bolts, visible on the western side, as part of the restoration.

Detail from the timeline on the causeway.

John Loveday established several limes in his gardens, although the only significant ones seen today are 90–100 year old replacements on the eastern boundary (Church Road side). In winter the mistletoe growing high in the branches is clearly visible. A line of limes existed on the western side of the causeway, and they are replicated by this modern row planted and trained in the pleached style. The trees are within the allotment and only the tops are visible from the causeway to the gazebo.

In the spring following the death of his daughter Mary, John decided to do something with the garden. As we saw with his father Thomas, and his grandfather Thomas senior, the Lovedays never followed fashions in house improvements or garden development, but in that spring of 1750, John decided there was a need for some remedial work. He had discovered that there were many snails living contentedly in the high wall between the gardens and the church, and that they were causing much damage. He arranged for as many of them as possible to be destroyed at a cost of two pence per hundred, and later noted in his diary that 12,550 had been accounted for! That would have been a total cost of £1 0s 11d, about £195 at 2012 prices.

Later in the year he widened the path in his 'warren', which was formerly the Old Rectory rabbit warren, and now a road by the same name.

Sadly such dreams were short-lived. Their first son William was born and died in 1740, and in November 1743, a month after giving birth to a still-born daughter, Anna Maria also died. John's diary entry for 19 November read 'The Delight of my Eyes vanished to the Father of Spirits a minute after 6 in the Evening.' (Markham, 1984). Six years later, during which time John had re-married, to Dorothy 'Dolly' Bagshaw, further tragedy struck. Mary, his sole surviving daughter with Anna Maria, died at school at Dorchester, and was buried in the family vault in St Peter's early in December 1749.

In 1756 John married his third wife, Penelope Forrest, his second having died a year earlier. This partnership resulted in a further son and five daughters, the second of whom, Penelope, was to maintain her father's tradition of copious diary and letter writing. This quality was also demonstrated by Jack Loveday, the sole surviving son of John and Anna Maria. He followed in his father's footsteps to Magdalen College at Oxford, later became a lawyer, and brought his wide circle of friends to Caversham in the same way John had done years before. Jack even went travelling with his father, joining him on his last tour of 1765.

John's remaining years were spent in Caversham in the company of an increasing number of young people, and as ever, the doors of the Striped House were always open to visitors.

In March 1789, not long before he died, John wrote the following by way of adapting some lines

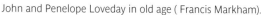

John and Penelope Loveday in old age (Francis Markham).

from Alexander Pope which 'aptly delineate some circumstance attending J.L. and his mansion at Caversham'. (Markham, 1984)

> *'Let me on Thames's banks recline at ease,*
> *And see what friends, and read what books I please;*
> *I was not born for courts or great affairs;*
> *I pay my debts, believe, and say my prayers.'*

In April 1791, John's son, Jack, took out insurance on the property in Caversham, together with some of the contents. It is interesting to see that whilst the 'Parsonage House' was valued at £1250, the 'printed books only in said ... house ...' were valued at £500, and 'plate herein ...' was £100 (LMA LC/B/192/F/001/ MS11936/377/582266). This clearly shows the value of the library which had been collected largely by John Loveday senior during his lifetime.

Eight years later the house was put up for sale, Jack having previously moved with his family to Warwickshire.

Henry John Simonds (1828–1896)

Henry John Simonds, nephew of Blackall, moved into the property in 1866 before inheriting it from his uncle in 1875. The impact this event had on the local community is reported in the *Reading Mercury* when the Simonds family made a triumphal entrance into the house, now being referred to as the 'Rectory' rather than the 'Old Rectory'.

> Caversham. —This pretty village was the scene of some festivity on Tuesday last, when H. Simonds, Esq., and H. J. Simonds, Esq., and family took possession of their new residence—the Rectory, which property had been let for a period of more than 20 years. The Rectory has undergone considerable repairs and decoration and on the arrival of the family on Tuesday the workmen and the others assembled in front of the house and gave enthusiastic cheers as the carriage drove under a brilliant triumphal arch which had been erected near the entrance gate. In the evening the workmen were most liberally entertained at supper and the healths of the various members of the family were drunk with great cheering (The *Reading Mercury*, 11 August 1866).

Census records show that the house was enlarged between 1871 and 1891, particularly after Henry John's second marriage in 1875. A billiard room, fernery and extra accommodation were added. After the repeal of the glass tax in the mid-nineteenth century it was less expensive to build garden glasshouses and as a result there was a rise in the

The Hop Leaf Gazette.

The Monthly Journal of H. & G. SIMONDS, Ltd.

Edited by CHARLES H. PERRIN.

No. 10.   JULY   1927.

The Late Mr. HENRY JOHN SIMONDS.

Henry John Simonds (1828–1896), brewer, scholar, lawyer and friend of the Prime Minister, William Gladstone. He played cricket for his college and once for England.

cultivation of tender and exotic vegetables, fruit and plants. The glasshouses and supporting buildings were described in the 1909 sales particulars for the house as: 'Peach House, about 50 yards long, Palm House, 45ft by 21ft, Early and late Vineries, Tomato and Melon Houses, Forcing pits, Potting and Tool Sheds, Carpenter's Shop etc.'

Late medieval, *c.*1450

Tudor, *c.*1530

Elizabethan, *c.*1580

Elizabethan, *c.*1600

Jacobean, *c.*1630

Regency, *c.*1800

Victorian, *c.*1880

DRAWING ROOM

DINING ROOM

(WINE CELLAR BELOW)

STUDY

'MONK'S HOLE' BELOW

MAIN STAIRCASE

LIGHT WELL

BILLIARD ROOM

CORRIDOR HALL

STAIRCASE HALL

(BEER CELLARS BELOW)

FERNERY

CELLAR STEPS

ENTRANCE HALL

YARD

KITCHEN

SCULLERY

SERVANTS' HALL

BUTLER'S PANTRY

BACK STAIRS

LARDER

UPPER NORTH WING ABOVE

The additions of the fernery and billiard room by Henry John Simonds can be seen on the ground floor house plan. The reception rooms were on the south side of the house, overlooking the river, and the servants' quarters were at the back close to the kitchen gardens and stables.

Several servants lived in the house, with others coming in from the village daily, such as gardeners, coachmen and those who worked in the laundry and brewhouse situated close to the house (Reading Borough Council, 2009).

View across the roof of the enlarged Simonds house c.1890. The roof of the billiard room can be seen in the foreground. In the background is Caversham bridge, constructed in iron in 1869 to replace the increasingly unsafe medieval bridge. In 1926 the iron bridge was in turn replaced by the current structure.

By 1890 the house had also acquired a veranda, as remembered by Marianne Loveday on a visit in 1890: 'Along the front of the house was a delightful verandah covered with awning, under which on a very wide paved terrace were tables and chairs, a sort of out-door drawing room' (Markham and Arnold 1973).

Celebratory bridal arch at the bottom of Church Road, looking towards Bridge Street, for the wedding of Helen Isabel Simonds (aged about 17 years) to Francis Caulfeild on 11 November 1880 at St Peter's Church, Caversham.

The present-day herbaceous border beneath the long walk at the end nearest to the house footprint recreates the style of Victorian-Edwardian planting. In April and May the bronze iris and poppies are in bloom against a green background and catmint, golden marjoram and box provide colour and shape along the front. In the 1880s and 1890s flowers in the garden under cover and outside included lantana, cyclamen, primula, calceolaria, cineraria, gloxinia, and pelargoniums.

The lifestyle of Henry John at the Rectory reflected the tastes and fashionable pursuits of a wealthy and successful member of local society. He was Mayor of Reading and a Justice of the Peace in 1866. From the 1870s onwards he hosted the Reading Regatta, and as they strolled about the lawns his guests drank champagne which had been cooled in the cellars situated underneath the kitchen. Four of his daughters, Helen Isabel, Mary Amelia, Isa Florence and Lillian Julietta were married from the house between 1880 and 1891, and these weddings were important society events in the local area. His youngest child and his heir, born in 1867, was given the distinctive name of Henry Caversham Simonds.

Gardeners and glasshouses

Mrs Monck's gardener was William Jacob, a Caversham man who began as one of her live-in servants in 1851 and who was head gardener in a tied house in Buckside in 1861. He managed the kitchen garden, the pleasure garden and the conservatory. His successful entries in the local flower shows in the 1860s reflect the popularity of roses at a time when new hybrid tea varieties were being introduced.

When Henry John Simonds took possession of his house in 1866 he appointed his own more experienced gardener, Charles Lanaway, who had previously worked for the architect Alfred Waterhouse. Immediately the show results suggest that the style of the garden had changed. Competition between the professional gardens in local estates was very strong. A winning entry was good for the status of the house and its owner, and the prize money was a valuable addition to the gardener's wages.

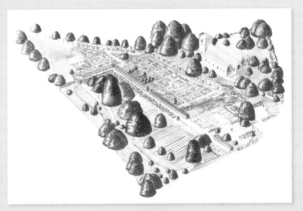

This map from the display boards in the gardens shows the extent of the working gardens, their position relative to the house and to the brick walls and yew hedges protecting them (Reading Borough Council, 2009).

READING HORTICULTURAL SOCIETY

Mr Charles Lanaway, gardener to Mr H.J. Simonds Esq. Caversham

One side of the upper slopes [of the site] was filled with groups of mixed plants for artistic arrangement, each group occupying 12ft by 10ft. The group of Mr Lanaway … was exceedingly beautiful, and the border of moss and flowers added considerably to the beauty of the group. Two figs – prize to Mr C Lanaway. Six ferns in 6in pots suitable for table decoration, second prize to Mr Lanaway

(*Reading Mercury*, 27 August 1870)

In 1882 George Parham, aged 46, previously gardener at Sidmouth House in Reading, placed an advertisement in the Situations Wanted column of the local paper; the experience that he was offering was what Mr Simonds needed to manage his garden and glasshouses to a high standard, and he was taken on at the Rectory.

GARDENER (HEAD) where four or more are kept; 20 years' experience as above; understands vines, orchids, stove and greenhouse plants, kitchen, fruit, and flower garden; 13 years' in present situation. Address G. Parham, 35, The Grove, Reading

(*Reading Mercury*, 4 March 1882)

The head gardener was one of the senior staff in the house, equal in importance to the butler and the cook, with both of whom he worked closely in keeping the house and conservatory filled with flowers for the pleasure of family and visitors, the kitchens supplied and the dining tables decorated. Successful men of this time wanted their wealth to be seen in their houses and gardens and in their generous level of entertaining. Guests would be invited to enjoy the conservatory, to see the kitchen or productive garden and to walk through the orchid house, the vinery and the fernery.

A view of the Victorian house showing the two-sectioned circular conservatory and rectangular vinery in the pleasure gardens.

In Victorian times the kitchen garden took up the space now occupied by the present-day allotments and the canoe club. The garden was warmed on one side by the brick wall (now a Grade II listed structure) whose deep bays stored and radiated heat to ripen fruit, and it was sheltered from wind damage by the yew hedge on the opposite side.

The productive garden was on the side of the house closest to the kitchens and pantries, and the head gardener supplied the kitchen and dining room every day of the year with fruit and vegetables according to season and as required for entertaining. He planted early and late crops, forced and held back others so that there was a steady supply to the kitchen of the usual root vegetables, of cauliflower, broccoli and sprouts, peas and beans, herbs and salads for the table. Seasonal crops such as rhubarb, asparagus and celery added variety. He grew soft fruits as cordons to edge the paths and raised strawberries, melons, cucumbers and tomatoes under glass. Selected varieties of apples, pears, plums, apricots and figs on the brick walls would have given fruit throughout the summer season and, once picked and stored, the supply lasted into the winter.

The garden wall, about 75 m long, with its 14 curved bays facing south, still holds the hand-made nails that were used to fix the metal frames against which the fruit trees were trained. It is not a classic crinkle-crankle wall because it is more than one brick deep and it has buttresses to support it. In the distance to the left on the photograph is part of the long wall that runs towards the canoe club. The pillars in the wall are hollow and worked as heating ducts, fed from a boiler, to keep the wall and the houses warm, so allowing peaches and apricots to ripen.

Above: The site of the conservatory and vinery was uncovered during the restoration of the Gardens. In the far wall the bricked-up entrance to the potting shed and boiler room which housed the pump have emerged from under the mound of earth that had long been covering them.

Right: The coal for the boiler was delivered from the road into a small cellar, and this point is marked on the top by a brick chimney added during the recent restoration. The pond has been rebuilt. There is now a new frame, but without glass, and an outdoor variety of grape, *Vitis vinifera 'Purpurea'* is being trained to cover it. The plantings here are a reminder that house plants may have been raised or overwintered under glass.

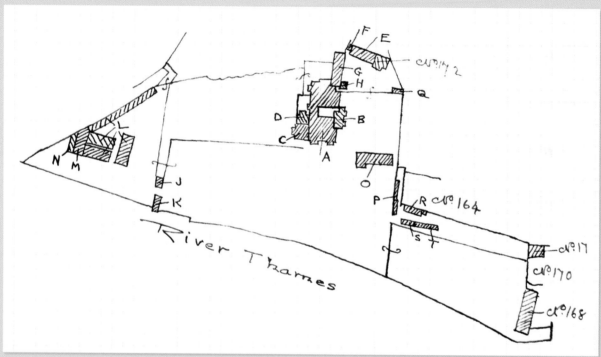

This plan, a page from an Inland Revenue's enumerator's note book, shows the positions of the various Victorian glasshouses that were still on the site in 1910. A, B and C mark parts of the house; D is the brick and glass fernery; E, F, G, H, and Q are coach houses, stabling and dog kennels; J and K are the summer house and boathouse; L marks four glasshouses; M the palmery, and N the potting shed; O the vinery and P, R, S and T are glasshouses and frames. Nos 164 and 172 are outbuildings listed separately (TNA, IR 58/68919).

Some more of the glasshouses in the kitchen garden in the 1920s.

A botanical drawing of Mr Parham's specimen orchid *Vanda teres*.

It was with the glasshouse plants that the mid-Victorian head gardener came into his own in competitions, and as the plan shows, the garden was well-equipped. Mr Parham's early successes were in the Reading Chrysanthemum Society show in 1884 and 1885. Chrysanthemums were grown in unheated glasshouses and used to decorate conservatories. Japanese varieties were large and showy, with big heads, and had their own classes. The results here also give the prize money graded for different classes, according to the degree of difficulty of producing blooms. Mr Parham earned that day a total of £ 7 15s, more than twice his weekly wage.

READING CHRYSANTHEMUM SOCIETY

Mr Parham gardener to Mr H.J. Simonds Reading:
Best collection of plants grown in pots, 50sq ft, equal third prize 20s; Six distinct varieties, Japanese excluded, third prize 40s; Six Japanese distinct varieties; third prize 30s; Three standards distinct varieties third prize 10s; Three cyclamen first prize 10s; One pot of violets first prize 5s; Two *Epiphyllum truncatum* [Christmas cactus] first prize 10s; One Tree Fern; first prize 30s

(*Reading Mercury*, 21 November 1885)

In the Reading Horticultural Society's show that year the judge described Mr Parham's *Dendrobium devonianum*, a specimen stove or greenhouse plant with attractive foliage or flowers, for which he had first prize, as being a rare orchid, having 500 flowers, sepals white with purple spots and with an orange centre. His specimen orchid, *Vanda teres*, brought him a second prize. One of the glasshouses on the heated wall was a palm house, a status symbol of its time and a place to take guests, where tropical and subtropical plants like palms and bamboo were grown. In this same show he took a first prize for three palms as well as gloxinias, which could be used to make a bright underplanting on the staging.

The nineteenth century was a time of 'fern fever' as new species were brought into the country by plant hunters, and all the best gardens had displays of these fashionable plants and entered them in flower shows. As early as 1866 Sutton's catalogue offered more than 130 species of ferns. At the Rectory the fernery was added to the west side of the house, separated from it by a glass door, where it could be enjoyed by the occupants and managed by the garden staff without disrupting the household. It was designed to show plants growing under glass in a natural style by planting them among stones and cascades of water, and it had to be tall enough to take tree ferns.

At this time the 'stones' in many ferneries and grottos were made by James Pulham and Sons, and were a porous light-weight rock substitute. Later sales particulars for the Rectory say that the fernery had 'imitation rock walls and cascades' and this suggests they were of similar construction. Reports from the Reading Flower Show and the Reading Horticultural Show in 1887 show that Mr Parham was producing high quality plants in the fernery and the palm house.

Gymnogramme elegantissima. This plant belongs to the Gold and Silver Ferns, 'the underneath of the foliage of many of them covered in farina [powder] of a colour varying from the purest white to shades of yellow of different degrees of intensity'. Some were white and yellow at the same time. The gardeners used them in hanging baskets in the greenhouse or fernery to fill the headspace and to display them to their best advantage (Geo Nicholson *Dictionary of Gardening* Div XI p408 fig 430).

READING FLOWER SHOW

Mr H.J. Simonds was a good third [in the 10ft by 12ft class], a magnificent tree fern overhanging a mass of very bright azaleas having a charming effect. There were three competitors in the stove and greenhouse class and Mr Parham scored a notable victory with a collection including [tree ferns] *Davallia moorcana*, *Asophila australis* and *Cibotrum Schiedei*. Foliage plants were again first class, Mr. Parham again winning with a collection including a really good palm … Mr. Parham again won in exotic ferns or mosses. Six stove plants: first prize; Specimen orchid: first prize; Group of plants 10×12ft: third prize; Six stove or greenhouse ferns: first prize; Six variegated foliage plants: first prize; Fifteen exotic ferns or mosses: second prize

(*Reading Mercury*, 4 June 1887)

In 1888 it was William Henry Willis, aged 34 and a thoroughly experienced gardener, who placed an advertisement in the Situations Wanted column of the local paper. He was taken on at the Rectory and took prizes in 1892 for apricots and for stove plants in flower; in 1893 for lilies; in 1894 for stove or greenhouse ferns; and in 1895 for tree ferns and palms, stove plants including orchids, and for cinerarias and primulas. He was still in post in 1896 when Henry John Simonds died, and he continued as head gardener when Henry Caversham Simonds took over the house in 1897. He was still submitting entries to the shows in the early 1900s.

Henry Caversham Simonds (1867–1918)

The Hop Leaf Gazette.

The Monthly Journal of
H. & G. SIMONDS, Ltd.

Edited by CHARLES H. PERRIN.

No. 9.   JUNE   1927.

The Late COLONEL H. CAVERSHAM SIMONDS.
See next page.

Henry Caversham Simonds (1867–1918).

Henry Caversham Simonds inherited the Rectory in 1896 and for a few years continued to host glamorous social gatherings there. The requirements of society living also necessitated owning horses and carriages and employing coachmen and stable lads. The house gained a turning circle for carriages, and visitors to the Gardens nowadays will see a large flower urn where formerly the Simonds family had placed a font in the middle of the circle.

The kitchen maid recalled that during Ascot week in 1897 servants produced picnics tied up with blue ribbons, which included soup, chicken, duck, game, fish, potatoes cooked in four different ways, trifles, gateaux, jellies and champagne. The party would leave in a horse and carriage and return for a dance in the evening.

Henry Caversham also entertained the South Berks Hunt on the lawns and terraces of the Old Rectory. He enjoyed competitive riding and showing horses that he had bred and entering them into steeplechases. Together with his gardener Mr Willis, he continued to produce winning flower specimens. However, this lifestyle was not destined to continue indefinitely and it became apparent that money had to be raised. This was done by selling assets from the Old Rectory Estate. In 1903 an auction was advertised to sell building land near the police station in Church Road, and Henry Caversham moved out, putting the house up for sale in 1909 and again in 1911. He continued to sell off land and buildings piecemeal until his death in 1918.

A view of the lawn from the river with the blue atlas cedar
(*Cedrus atlantica Glauca*) in front of the long east border.

Looking this time from the lawn towards the river with the Cedar
of Lebanon (*Cedrus libani*) in the centre. The redwood and the copper
beech on the lawn further to the west of the cedar, and the mulberry
inside the main gate, are among oldest trees in the garden and date
from the Simonds family's occupancy of the property.

Public Gardens in the 1930s

Caversham in the 1930s was still close to rural greenery and was well provided with riverside walks. In turning Caversham Court into a public garden, Reading Corporation gave Caversham a unique open space which became even more precious as the area became built-up.

Postcard entitled 'Caversham Court Gardens', by H.A. Giles, c.1930. Part of the gardens looking east and showing a herbaceous border and stepped path in crazy paving descending a grassy bank.

Below: The tea kiosk, by Caversham artist Mary Phelan (2011). The Arts and Crafts style tea kiosk began life as a toilet block, built when the Gardens were opened to the public in the 1930s. It was constructed using some of the rubble from the demolished main house. Now refashioned to include a kitchen area, the tea kiosk is run by a number of local charities.

Caversham Court in World War II (1939–1945)

This photograph was obviously displayed in an exhibition, bearing the typewritten caption 'Reading 1945, dancing in Caversham Court' (REDMG:1946.52.246).

Leading Fireman Arthur 'Happy' Adsolom is shown here with members of the AFS team in 1940.

During World War II the Gardens were a popular venue for theatricals and entertainment. As early as 1940 the former kitchen gardens were offered as allotments and used as part of the Dig for Victory campaign. 'Holidays at Home' entertainments in Caversham Court included the Ballet Rambert and Shakespeare plays, and such entertainments continued throughout the twentieth century.

The Auxiliary Fire Service (AFS) was based at Caversham Court during World War II. This was a volunteer group created in 1938 to provide part-time assistance to the fire brigade in wartime. It merged with the regular fire brigades in 1941 to form the

He put the letters AFS in cement on a brick at the back of the garages.

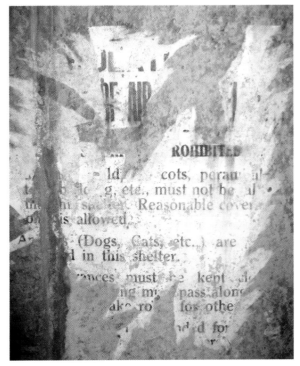

The 'Stanton' air raid shelter, made out of concrete sections, now houses Thames Water hydraulics equipment. It still bears a poster warning people not to bring pets down into the shelter and traces of graffiti where two sixteen-year-olds inscribed their names and an arrow piercing a heart, dated 24 April, 1944.

National Fire Service. One of the volunteer firemen recalled that the old garages at Caversham Court were used for the water pumps and vehicles – there were no fire engines, only cars requisitioned from civilians (Sandall, 1993).

Caversham was spared serious damage in World War II, though a number of incendiary bombs hit the village centre. A lone German aircraft strafed Hemdean Road on 3 February 1943, causing damage to houses and to Hemdean Road School (now Caversham Primary). Just a week later, on 10 February 1943, Reading town centre suffered its worst air raid of the war when the People's Pantry and other buildings in the Market Place were hit; 41 people were killed and over 100 injured. The Caversham fire-fighters would certainly have been on duty that day.

Mayor of Reading Fred Pugh leads excited children into the newly-refurbished Gardens on 7 August 2009. The impressive stone battlemented entrance leading to Church Road is a faithful copy of the grand entrance to the Victorian mansion.

allows the people of Reading to enjoy a peaceful and beautiful retreat near the town centre. This enjoyment includes raising public awareness of the heritage, cultivating the Gardens to both encourage urban wildlife and display horticultural excellence, and providing a sense of safety' (Reading Borough Council, 2012).

Looking north towards St. Peter's Church and over the western border, from the lawns beneath the beech tree. A fine summer morning in July.

Designing a planting scheme for the restored Gardens presented various challenges. The gardens at Caversham Rectory were not the work of any great designer. They are interesting precisely because they evolved in response to the fashions of the time and the interests of the owners.

Their history is therefore a story of the activities and preferences of the upper middle classes over several centuries. This means that there was no particular date back to which the Gardens should be restored. The planting design tries to capture something of their evolution, and to continue the process into the twenty-first century.

Although the Gardens are now in public ownership, intended for the enjoyment of all, they retain the sense of intimacy of a private garden. It is important that each area of the Garden achieves its own sense of place at a domestic scale. At the same time, the Gardens can be viewed from a distance, both across the river and down from St Peter's churchyard. They therefore must be successful as a canvas, where the overall composition harmonises the elements.

The colours and textures of the beech tree (left), and Californian redwood tree (right) contrast with the grass below, and frame the river Thames.

Iris germanica 'Kent Pride', at its best in the eastern border in late May.

The existing trees and historic structures are both constraints and opportunities. Nowhere is this more a consideration than below the long walk, where the western border is shaded by large trees. One design for the whole border would never work, because only a section would thrive. This problem was solved by planting a formal seventeenth-century display along the western border, and nineteenth-century luxuriance along the sun-drenched eastern border. The twenty-first-century preoccupation with colour, form and ecology is captured by the planting on the lavender bank.

The Gardens must give pleasure in all seasons. The winter walk is carefully designed to be fragrant and colourful during the winter months for the pedestrian commuters who daily traverse the path between the churchyard and the main gate. Early spring bulbs under the yew family and along the lower lawn are intended to tempt strollers deeper into the gardens as the winter draws to a close. The borders are stocked with a succession of flowering plants from spring until autumn, but are at their most lovely in high summer.

A solitary poppy provides a striking counterfoil to the silver foliage of the eastern border, also in late May.

71

Caversham Court Today

Caversham Court today is a well-loved spot, popular with young and old alike. The Friends of Caversham Court Gardens run an Easter Egg Trail for children on Easter Saturday, and join with the choir of St Peter's church for candle-lit carols in the Gardens before Christmas. Reading's Progress Theatre stages a Shakespeare play each summer, and the parish fête is a firm favourite in July, along with many other community and commercial events. A highlight of 2012 was the Olympic Torch Relay, which emerged from the gazebo to start its way through Reading on Day 54 of its route round Britain.

Above, below and bottom right: Visitors relax with family and friends on sunny summer days but also come into the Gardens throughout the year.

Immediate right: Visitors explore the footprint to learn more of the layout of Caversham Court.

Above: Members of the Reading Scottish Pipe Band pose for a photo with Olympic torchbearer Bob Tutton from Purley, who ran through Yeovil in 1948 as well as running in the 2012 relay in Windsor. The Pipe Band provided entertainment for the large crowds awaiting the Olympic Torch Relay in Caversham Court Gardens and later went on to perform at the Olympics closing ceremony in August. Torchbearer Lee Umpleby set off from the Gazebo to begin the relay through Caversham on 11 July 2012.

How the gardens grew

January

A cloudless sky. White blocks dazzle as I pace
the footprint of the house, decipher
ground-set plaques: kitchen, pantry, library.
Mistletoe clings to the branches
of the roadside limes. The river's bare of craft
but geese slip by on ruffled images.
An east wind rattles sedum heads, slides inside
my padded hood. I read the panelled history
through half-shut eyes, am numb to the prayers
of ancient occupants, the weight of lives
sheltered by brick and flint.

July

A faltering sun. From the churchyard I look down
on scrambling runner beans, freighted
apple-trees; on cosmos, alliums. The bank
billows with santolina, lavender – ivory,
purple, gold. Mossed walls by the Long Walk
crawl with clematis, wisteria; back flossy spires
of plume poppies. Penstemons sprawl
among cardoons; bees and hoverflies fizz
and bounce; the griffins' snarls are fiercer
in new paint. Above the cronk of ducks,
there's the knock and slosh of oars,
the rhythmic chanting of a cox.
Now I can hear the clamour of the past.

Gill Learner

Visiting the Gardens

Location

The Gardens are located on the A4074 (Church Road), a short walk from Caversham Bridge, RG4 7AG. The main entrance is between The Griffin pub and St Peter's Church.

Buses 22, 24, 27, and X39/X40 all go over Caversham Bridge and stop on Bridge Street.

Opening times

The gardens are open during daylight hours every day of the year except Christmas Day.

Further information

http://home.fccg.org.uk
http://www.theteakiosk.org.uk

Facilities & access

- Limited parking is available on The Warren. There is a bike rack inside the main gates.
- Parking for disabled visitors is situated at the main gates in Church Road.
- There is wheelchair access to and throughout the gardens.
- There are also toilets and accessible toilets, with baby-changing facilities.
- The tea kiosk sells teas, coffee and home-made cakes in aid of local charities. It is open from March to November, on Tuesdays to Sundays and on Bank Holidays, 11 am to 5 pm. In the summer months of June to August it is open until 6 pm.
- You are welcome to bring a picnic, but please do not light barbecues.
- Dogs on leads are welcome.

Sources and image credits

Primary sources

LMA   London Metropolitan Archives
TNA   The National Archives

LMA, COL/AC/17/571
   Orphans inventory Roll 1863: inventory of the
   personal estate of Thomas Loveday
LMA, CLC/B/192/F/001/MS11936/377/582266
   Insurance agreement: John Loveday, of
   Caversham Oxfordshire, LLD, 1791 Apr 13
Reading Borough Council, *Caversham Court
Gardens Management and Maintenance Plan
April 2009–March 2019*, updated January 2012
TNA, C43/8/163
   Mylward alias Alexander v Brigham;
   C2/ELIZ/B25/42, Brigham v Alexander alias
   Milward 1558–1603
TNA, PROB 11/130 Will of Katherine Alexander
   alias Mylwarde widow of Caversham 1617
TNA, IR 58/68919 Inland Revenue survey
   Caversham 1910

On-line sources

http://www.crsbi.ac.uk
   *Corpus of Romanesque Sculpture in Britain and
Ireland*
http://www.johnlovedayofcaversham.co.uk
http://www.oakhillpekingese.com/Caversham.pdf
   Tony Rosato, *Footprints in the Breed: The
Caversham Pekingese*, January 2007

http://www.simondsfamily.me.uk
   *H&G Simonds Ltd: the story of the Bridge Street
Brewery Reading 1785–1980* (first published in 1980
as T. Corley, *The Road to Worton Grange: Simonds'
and Courage's brewery at Reading 1785–1980*)

Secondary sources

Jennifer Davies, *The Victorian Kitchen Garden*,
   BBC 1987
Sarah Markham, *John Loveday of Caversham 1711–1789:
The Life and Tours of an Eighteenth-Century Onlooker*,
   Michael Russell 1984
Sarah Markham, *A Testimony of her Times: based on
Penelope Hind's diaries and correspondence, 1787–1838*,
   Michael Russell 1990
Sarah Markham, *The Tours of John Loveday
of Caversham 1728 to 1765. Transcribed from
the original documents by Sarah Markham*,
   unpublished 2010
Sarah Markham and Godwin Arnold, *A history of
Caversham Court*, Reading Gazebo Trust and
   Reading Civic Society 1973
Geo. Nicholson FLS (ed), *The Illustrated Dictionary of
Gardening: An encyclopaedia of horticulture*
Reading Public Libraries, *Mayors of Reading: Fourteenth
to Twentieth Centuries*, 1970
Alan G. Sandall, *Are you 17?*, Alan Sandall of Frome
   1993

Further reading

Caversham 100 Years On, *Caversham 100 years on – Local Heritage Exhibitions* 2011

Gillian Clark, *Down by the River: the Thames and Kennet in Reading*, Two Rivers Press 2009

T.A.B Corley, 'Simonds' Brewery at Reading 1760–1960', *Berks Archaeological Journal*, vol 68, pp 77–88

Claude Hitchings, *Rock Landscapes – the Pulham legacy*, Antique Collectors Club 2012

Toby Musgrave, *The Head Gardeners*, London 2007

Sarah Whittingham, *Fern Fever: The story of Pteridomania*, Frances Lincoln 2012

Thanks are due to the following for access to documents and for permission to publish these illustrations:

David Arathoon

p. 56 Edward George Handel Lucas, portraits of Thaddeus and Mary Arathoon

Berkshire Record Office

p. 37 D/EX 965/16 Stable yard and coachman's cottage

p. 54 D/EX 965/12/1 Front entrance of the Rectory

p. 54 D/EX 965/13 Reading Philanthropic Society 1918

p. 57 D/EX 965/18/1 The gazebo and roof of boathouse

p. 60 D/EX 965/15 Demolition of the Rectory

p. 60 D/EX 965/21 Stones from the Rectory garden

p. 64 D/EX 965/13 Staircase and ceiling of the Rectory

Anne Keenan

p. 23 Gazebo in a ruinous state, January 2007

John and Lindsey Mullaney

p. 40 View 1865 from St Peter's across the Rectory

p. 44 Arch marking the wedding of Helen Isabel Simonds to Francis Caulfeild, both from *Life in Old Caversham* by Mary Kift

John Markham

p. 28 Schwartz, *Portrait of John Loveday age 10*, 1721

Francis Markham

p. 32 Miniature portraits of John and Penelope Loveday in old age. Artist unkown

Palmer Museum of Art of The Pennsylvania State University

p. 21 Thomas Murray, *Portrait of Thomas Loveday*, c. 1705. Oil on canvas, 76.4 × 64.1 cm. 2005.62

p. 21 Thomas Murray, *Portrait of Sarah Lethieullier Loveday*, c. 1705. Oil on canvas, 75.2 × 62.6 cm. 2005.63

p. 29 Thomas Gibson, *Portrait of John Loveday*, 1739. Oil on canvas, 64 × 76 cm. 2005.64

Reading Borough Council

p. 5 Plan of Caversham Court Gardens. Base image produced 2009

p. 17 Ground floor plan of the Loveday Old Rectory House. Produced 2009

p. 18 First floor plan of the Loveday Old Rectory House. Produced 2009

p. 42 Ground floor plan of the Simonds House. Produced 2009

p. 45 Map from the display boards. Produced 2009.

p. 55 Letter from Lady Mosley to Thaddeus Arathoon 1918

p. 59 Estate map Caversham Court 1927

Reading Museum

Copyright Reading Museum (Reading Borough Council). All rights reserved

p. 13 REDMG:1971.86 Newel post from Caversham Court staircase, found in the stables

p. 25 REDMG:1998.180.53 Edmund Havell Snr watercolour *Thames at Caversham 1825*

p. 59 REDMG:1997.150.193 The south front of Caversham Court overlooking the terraced lawn 1932, one of a group of five images

p. 59 REDMG:1997.150.193 The main entrance of Caversham Court 1932, one of a group of five images

p. 62 REDMG:1946.52.246 Holidays at home: Sunday afternoon Morris dancing display on the lawn

p. 65 REDMG:2002.89.2 Plasterwork ceiling decoration from Caversham Court featuring part of a coat of arms with three dogs' heads in a shield

Reading Local Studies Library

p. 16 Charles Tomkins, detail from *View of Caversham Through the Gateway 1791*

p. 34 *London Illustrated News* 30 August 1884

p. 38 *The Hop Leaf Gazette* no. 13, October 1927 Mr Blackall Simonds

p. 41 *The Hop Leaf Gazette* no. 10 July 1927 Mr Henry John Simonds

p. 43 Francis Frith and and Company, Horizon no. 120596 St Peter's Church, Caversham, Reading, and the Old Rectory from across the river, c. 1890

p. 43 H.W. Taunt, Horizon no. 1238588. View from St. Peter's Church, Caversham looking towards Caversham Bridge and Reading, c. 1900 [sic]

p. 46 RH/NW 1909 sales catalogue South front of the Rectory

p. 51 *The Hop Leaf Gazette* no. 9 June 1927 Mr Henry Caversham Simonds

p. 61 H.A. Giles. Horizon no. 1225831 postcard entitled 'Caversham Court Gardens', c. 1930, showing a herbaceous border and stepped path in crazy paving descending a grassy bank

p. 66 Francis Frith and Company, ref cvm2. Horizon no. 1204956. Gardens border, probably 1950s, showing the strawberry tree, with the yew hedge behind

p. 66 Francis Frith and and Company, ref cvm1. Horizon no. 1204740. St Peter's Church, Caversham, from the south *c.* 1950

Reading Post

p. 66 *Reading Standard*, 6 July 1956. Children's Festival advertisement

Raymond Simonds

p. 33 Portraits of William Blackall Simonds and Elizabeth Blackall Simonds

The National Archives

p. 10 c2/eliz/b25/42 Thomas Brigham v William Alexander alias Milward 1558–1603

p. 48 ir 58/68919 plot 167 Inland Revenue survey Caversham 1910

University of Reading, Museum of English Rural Life

p. 27 p dx 323 e45/121 Wet boat house at Caversham Court

p. 50 Geo. Nicholson FLS (ed), *The Illustrated Dictionary of Gardening: An encyclopaedia of horticulture*, Div XI p. 408, fig. 430 *Gymnogramme elegantissima*. L. Upcot Gill (undated)

Every effort has been made to trace owners of photographs or holders of copyright and the publishers would be grateful for further information on any sources inadvertently missed.

Two Rivers Press has been publishing in and about Reading
since 1994. Founded by the artist Peter Hay (1951–2003),
the press continues to delight readers, local and further afield,
with its varied list of individually designed, thought-provoking books.